Psalm 23
The Lord is My Shepherd

by:

M.A. Benjamin

Illustrated by:

Wilma McDaniel and
M.A. Benjamin

AuthorHouse™
1663 Liberty Drive
Bloomington, IN 47403
www.authorhouse.com
Phone: 833-262-8899

ISBN: 978-1-4567-5993-3 (sc)
ISBN: 978-1-7283-7153-5 (e)

Print information available on the last page.

Published by AuthorHouse 11/23/2020

authorHOUSE®

This book is dedicated to our grandchildren

Desteny G, Faith H, Anna M, Hope H
Xavier F, Janae H, Elijah P, Xalya F
Xandria F, Xander T, Ezekiel M

by: Desteny G.

CLOTHES

Milk

FOOD

FAMILY

LOVE

FUN

JOY

HAPPINESS

The LORD is My Shepherd, I shall not want,
(The LORD gives up everything we need.)

He makes me to lie down in green pastures:
he leads me besides the still waters.

He restores my soul: he leads me in the
paths of righteousness for his name's sake.
(If we ask He will guide us in whatever we do)

Even, though I walk through the valley
of the shadow of death, I will fear
no evil: for you art with me; your rod
and your staff they comfort me.
(you don't have to be afraid, the
LORD will always protect you)

The LORD prepares a table before you
in the presence of your enemies:
(The LORD always wants what is best for you)

The LORD anoints my head with
oil; my cup overflows.

Surely goodness and mercy shall
follow me all the days of my life:
(No matter how old you get Father
GOD wants to bless you.)

and I will live in the house of the LORD forever.

Prayer

Thank you GOD for guiding me and taking good care of me. Please keep helping me to be good, and help me to be really smart in school. Thank you. In Jesus name I pray. Amen.

Reference: PSALM 23. King James Version

Printed in the United States
By Bookmasters